Abba, Father

Our Journey into Father's Heart

I0201413

By Bob Mumford

LIFECHANGERS®

P.O. Box 3709 ❖ Cookeville, TN 38502
931.520.3730 ❖ lc@lifechangers.org

The Scripture quotations contained in this book are from:
The Amplified Bible. 1987. La Habra, CA: The Lockman
Foundation. *The New American Standard Bible*®, Copyright ©
1960, 1962, 1963, 1971, 1972, 1973, 1975, 1977, 1995 by The
Lockman Foundation.

PLUMBLINE

Published by:

P.O. Box 3709 | Cookeville, TN 38502
(800) 521-5676 | www.lifechangers.org

Abba Father
Our Journey into Father's Heart

Contents

Introduction

It was for freedom that Christ set us free (Gal. 5:1).

When we authentically love someone, our primary intent is to set them free. Father wants us to know His kind of forgiveness—the kind that sets us free internally. It is only when we are internally free that we have the capacity and desire to respond externally to God as a Father and demonstrate the ability to hear His voice.

The journey toward freedom often seems complex and difficult. My desire is to speak both to the complexity of the journey as well as the unavoidable need to embrace the journey. Personal freedom, as we shall see, is not an option. It is, by all scriptural determination, a prerequisite to our becoming a Father-pleaser.

God arranged for forgiveness to be freely made available; Jesus said to forgive 70 times 7—that is 490 times. Consequently, it should be evident that simply being forgiven cannot be the significant issue in the Kingdom. The complexity in forgiveness is that we are unfree. Compulsion and ungoverned desires control and govern us internally causing Jesus to ask, "Why do you call Me, 'Lord, Lord,' and do not do what I say?" (Luke 6:46). He was essentially saying, Why do you call Me Lord, when these other things are actually governing you?

However many times Father forgives, and He is eager to do so, He will never, ever cease moving us progressively and incrementally toward personal freedom. It is our personal freedom that facilitates our ability to hear His command and respond to Him with joy and alacrity!

Christ's job description, as stated in John 14:6, is to take us to the Father. That is an effective definition of the journey we are on and our personal freedom is a pre-requisite on this journey. Quite simply, refusal to grow up and embrace the journey toward freedom means we cannot become a Father-pleaser because we are too preoccupied with pleasing ourselves to know or bother pleasing Him! The trouble with most of us is that we have embraced a self-complex and are continuously going round in circles and coming back to the same point at which we started—everything centered on ourselves. This is unfree! When we are unfree, spiritual maturity doesn't have a chance. We must come to the end (Greek: telios) of ourselves.

Father Bringing Us to Himself

> *All that the Father gives Me will come to Me, and the one who comes to Me I will certainly not cast out (John 6:37).*

At the initial transgression explained in Genesis, all humanity entered a phase of personal focus that pre-empted our originally created Father-focus. So much of human complexity can be understood if we simply see the change in focus in a relational manner as contrasted with our usual doctrinal approach.

Father took the time and effort to meticulously explain that if we took this road of personal concern, it would lead to seeing ourselves as some kind of little god. This little god is easily offended and often scandalized at how and in what manner Father has chosen to govern His universe. Jesus informs us in direct appeal, "And blessed is he who does not take offense [be scandalized] at Me" (Matt. 11:6). People who have been scandalized are essentially unmanageable. Many are miserable simply because they cannot control God and make Him do what they think is reasonable!

As the result of the loss of our God-consciousness, we become captured and imprisoned by our own understanding. We know! And we know we are right! We are imprisoned in our certitude that is founded on erroneous and faulty pre-suppositions. Do not confuse me with the facts! Our certitude, both religious and philosophical, forms strongholds that are mental pre-suppositions that prevent us from knowing God. As a result, we are held in some kind of *eros* prison. It is much more problematic being self-deceived than having someone else cause our deception.

Father comes to us relationally in the Person of His Son in order to bring us to Himself. He works not with coercion or demand but with an offer of His love to bring us out of our self-made prison into His life of total freedom. His offer consists of proposing to be a Father to us, restoring the One we lost in the initial deception. Scripture identifies Father's appeal as persuasion (see 2 Cor. 6:18).

Without mental or emotional compulsion, Father begins to call us to Himself by means of His Son. He waits, sometimes years, for us to say: "I am persuaded…." With love and calculated appeal, He continually beckons us out of the tyranny and imprisonment of bondage to ourselves. He knows, even when we do not, that our freedom depends on being persuaded that Father desires our very best. This can be most complex and frightening because it exposes our limits, depicts our stubbornness, and reveals our self-deception. Not fun!

Father bases everything on faith. Carefully examined, faith is a most wonderful way of preserving our personal freedom. It is faith that provides for and facilitates the baby-steps that are honored by a caring Father Who never despises or rejects the feeblest attempt. He uses faith to make our journey to personal freedom in measured, incremental steps. Father never demands fruit out of season. He is the waiting Father!

Like a parent bird, Father carefully seeks opportunities to teach us to fly and get us out of the nest. We must fly if we are ever to be free! Like the disciples, we discover ourselves full of anxiety simply because we are in the boat; we must develop the ability to respond to the call to get out of the boat and walk on the water.

Father is a rewarder of those who are determined to find and know Him. He demonstrates that love in His Son. As any authentic parent will testify, giving His Son was more than giving Himself. He demonstrates His willingness and then rewards those who respond to His appeal and promise.

We are not and cannot be free as Father has intended until and unless we experience freedom from all forms of external government. Father chose to write His laws and desires internally—on the tablets of the human heart, so external laws and rules must be displaced and replaced by the internal aspects of His desire and intent. This may be radical, I know, and needs to be balanced in application, but it is accurate. Hebrews 7:19 states that "the Law never made anything perfect—but instead a better hope is introduced through which we [now] come close to God." The word "perfect" in Hebrews 7:19 means brought to full purpose. All internal governing presence is God's Own *Agape*. Father is inexorably moving toward our experiencing the freedom of being governed internally by that which pleases Him—His Own *Agape*. God is Agape. "For the love [*Agape*] of Christ controls and urges and impels us" (2 Cor. 5:14).

Rhema and Logos

Spiritual maturity consciously and unavoidably depends upon our having been instructed in both the full and apostolic foundation of written Scripture, i.e., the *logos* as well as the spoken word of God—the rhema. *Logos* is Strongs #3056, used 330 times in the New Testament. The *logos* foundation is summarized in Hebrews 6:1-3:

> *¹THEREFORE LET us go on and get past the elementary stage in the teachings and doctrine of Christ (the Messiah), advancing steadily toward the completeness and perfection that belong to spiritual maturity. Let us not again be laying the foundation of repentance and abandonment of dead works (dead formalism) and of the faith [by which you turned] to God, ²with teachings about purifying, the laying on of hands, the resurrection from the dead, and eternal judgment and punishment. [These are all matters of which you should have been fully aware long, long ago.] ³If indeed God permits, we will [now] proceed [to advance teaching].*

Rhema is Strong's #4487, used 68 times in the New Testament. Note Mary's response in Luke 1:37-38:

> ³⁷*For with God nothing is ever impossible and no word (spoken as compared to written word) from God shall be without power or impossible of fulfillment.* ³⁸*Then Mary said, Behold, I am the handmaiden of the Lord; let it be done to me according to what you have said. (God's spoken word through the angel). And the angel left her.*

Compare the use of both logos (written word) and rhema (spoken word) as used in the same verse Heb. 12:19-21:

> ¹⁹*And to the blast of a trumpet and a voice whose words make the listeners beg that nothing more be said to them.* ²⁰*For they could not bear the command that was given: If even a wild animal touches the mountain, it shall be stoned to death.* ²¹*In fact, so awful and terrifying was the [phenomenal] sight that Moses said, I am terrified (aghast and trembling with fear).*

We really do need to have a biblical foundation and a degree of maturity in order to lose our fear of God as a Father speaking to us. In *Exposition of Hebrews*, A. W. Pink describes the three uses of the term "word":

Three uses of Word; including rhema: The "worlds," or universe, were "framed," that is, were adjusted and disposed into a wise and beautiful order, by "the word of God." That expression is used in a threefold sense. **First**, there is the essential and personal Word, the eternal Son of God (John 1:1). **Second**, there is the written, ever-living Word, the Holy Scriptures (John 10:35). **Third**, there is the Word of Power or manifestation of the invincible will of God. It is the last-mentioned that is in view in Hebrews 11:3. The Greek for "word" is not "logos" (as in John 1:1), but "rhema" (as in Hebrews 1:3); "rhema" signifies a word spoken. **The reference is to God's imperial fiat. His effectual command,** as throughout Gen. 1: "God said (the manifestation of His invincible will) let light be, and light was." "For He spake, and it was done; He commanded and it stood fast" (Ps. 33:9). An illustration of the Word of His Power (see Hebrews 1:3) is found in John 5:28, 29. "So that things which are seen, were not made of things which do appear." There is some difficulty (in the Greek) in ascertaining the precise meaning of phrase. View in sight! **He who can call worlds into existence by the Word of**

His Power can command supplies for the neediest of His creatures.[1]

Mary, the mother of Jesus, was required to demonstrate freedom in order to yield to the word that was *spoken* regarding Father's request for her to embrace God's purpose. The freedom to which Father is calling us is *obligatory* and urgent because of the increasingly antagonistic climate and cultural circumstances in which we as westerners find ourselves.

Hebrews 6:1-3 asks that we allow ourselves to be *carried forward*—another word for mature— by refusing to be captured by the elementary and foundational teachings about Christ and His Kingdom. It encourages us to move toward advanced teaching—the freedom that will allow us to hear Father's voice, respond unafraid, and seek to accomplish that which He is expecting. This identifies the Father-pleaser that was demonstrated in the life, death, and resurrection of Jesus Christ. God wants to move us toward *Agape* maturity and the *freedom* that produces, enabling us to hear and respond! In this process we are conformed to the image of Jesus Christ—the One we are called to follow and whose job description is to take us to His Father.

A comprehensive understanding of the manner in which the Persons of the Godhead function in

[1]Pink, A. W. (1954). An exposition of Hebrews (642–643). Swengel, PA: Bible Truth Depot.

emphasis and not categories can be stated in biblical terms. Paul wants us to understand the over-all idea of accomplishing Father's goal of seeing that His will/wishes are accomplished in the earth (see Matt. 6:10). It sorts out like this: different gifts...one Spirit; different administrations... one Lord; different operations...one God. Every job description or particular function is fitted or included in the one governing reality of God's eternal purpose.

Christ as Father's Fullness

My intent in this section is to expand our understanding of the Person of Christ as the One assigned to take us to the Father. That is His job description. He identifies Himself as the Way (Strong's # 3598, used 101 times in the New Testament). Jesus is not the goal or the terminal point; He has never centered upon Himself; He is the Way to the Father. A small, paperback book entitled *The Forgotten Father*[2] is one of the best books on this subject. I encourage you to read it carefully. You will laugh and cry all the way through this life message from a wonderful, adventurous Anglican bishop who was powerfully used in the Charismatic movement. He, like others, could see that the entire movement was *corrupting* itself, losing its direction, and in our model, ceasing to see Jesus as the Way to the Father.

[2]Smail, Thomas. (1980). ISBN #0-340-25365-7.

In Scripture Christ is recorded as being the Father's *fullness*. Christ comes to fullness so that we, too, may come to fullness. He is more than and other than simply the Lamb that takes away the sin of the world! He takes away our sins in order to prepare us for the Father. Father is seeking people who want more than just going to Heaven; He seeks people who want to see His will accomplished in the earth. Note how Paul states both Christ's coming to fulness and our coming to fulness in these two verses:

> *9For in Him (Jesus Christ) the whole fullness of Deity (the Godhead) continues to dwell in bodily form [giving complete expression of the divine nature]. 10 And you are in Him, made full and having come to fullness of life [in Christ you too are filled with the Godhead — Father, Son and Holy Spirit — and reach full spiritual stature] (Col 2:9-10).*

Christ Jesus is the *source; the One appointed to take us to the Father and to instruct and impart to us that which He learned on His Own journey.* He wants to be involved with us on our own personal journey. Father has been pleased to allow this Son to reveal Him and make judgment calls on His behalf, and Father disallows anyone else to bring us to Him except this solitary Son. It is Christ Who has been *appointed* to bring us to the Father.

Christ is declared to be a full representation of the radiance of His *glory* and the full representation of His *character*. He is so much more than the Lamb Who forgives. Minimizing or reductionist application of Who Christ is does not honor Him. He has given Himself to us so that we can make a successful journey to personal freedom. As Bride and Bridegroom, He intends for us to do it together: He in us and we in Him!

God, as a Father, is *personally present* in Christ, reconciling the hurting world to Himself (see 2 Cor. 5:19). Christ, in turn, is *personally present* in us as His Bride, bringing us to Himself to prepare and then present to His Father.

The Scriptures declare that Christ and His Bride are a great mystery. And, it is a spiritual mystyery meaning we cannot perceive it apart from the New Birth because it is *meta-cognitive.* Entrance into the Kingdom dimension requires faculties of sight, hearing, feeling, and knowing that have been enhanced by the impartation of Christ's Own life entering our world by means of the DNA of God.

It is through Christ's role of *Bridegroom* that we have access to His personal, human spirit in order to be conformed into the image of His Own Person. Christ Jesus is that solitary, human being in Whom the pleasure of the Lord has been expressed (see Matt. 3:17, 17:5). *Only* Christ can make us able to *please* God.

Christ's Human Spirit

The job description of Jesus taking me to the Father has opened to the degree that has caused me to reel under the sheer implications. This, I will attempt to establish both scientifically and biblically. The basis of it comes from Jesus' prayer to the Father in John 17:18-26:

> *18Just as You sent Me into the world, **I also have sent them into the world.** 19And so for their sake and on their behalf I sanctify (dedicate, consecrate) Myself, that they also may be sanctified (dedicated, consecrated, made holy) in the Truth. 20Neither for these alone do I pray [it is not for their sake only that I make this request], but also for all those who will ever come to believe in (trust in, cling to, rely on) Me through their word and teaching, 21That they all may be one, [just] as You, Father, are in Me and I in You, that they also may be one in Us, so that the world may believe and be convinced that You have sent Me. 22I have given to them the glory and honor which You have given Me, that they may be one [even] as We are one: 23I in them and You in Me, in order that they may become one and perfectly united, that the world may know and [definitely] recognize that You*

*sent Me and that You have loved them [even] as You have loved Me. ²⁴Father, I desire that they also whom You have entrusted to Me [as Your gift to Me] may be with Me where I am, so that they may see My glory, which You have given Me [Your love gift to Me]; for You loved Me before the foundation of the world. ²⁵O just and righteous Father, although the world has not known You and has failed to recognize You and has never acknowledged You, I have known You [continually]; and these men understand and know that You have sent Me. ²⁶I have made Your Name known to them and revealed Your character and Your very Self, and I will continue to make [You] known, that the love which You have bestowed upon Me may be in them [felt in their hearts] and **that I [Myself] may be in them.***

In verse 18, Jesus states that as Father sent Him, so He sent us into the world. In the Greek this means to the same manner and degree. Christ was ever and always aware of His Father's *presence*— He was sent in Father's purpose and in the same manner sends us in Father's purpose. And, in the process, He gives us His presence in the equivalent manner that Father gave Himself to Christ.

Christ's obedience, sinlessness, consecration, suffering, and perfection was all accomplished in Him so that this same sequence would be and could be replicated in every one of us. If Jesus was made perfect by suffering, He would only use suffering to mature us in our own journey! When I read verse 26, "That I [Myself] may be in them," I knew there was a dimension of Christ's human spirit that has been made available to the Body of Christ and we have not understood or had the capacity/ability to draw upon it.

A Scientific Insight

Anyone who becomes seriously involved in the pursuit of science becomes convinced that there is a spirit manifest in the laws of the universe, a spirit vastly superior to that of man. ~Albert Einstein

All matter originates and exist only by virtue of a force; we must assume this force is the existence of a conscious and intelligent mind. This mind is the matrix of all matter. ~Max Planck, Father of Quantum Physics

It is to Christ's spirit and to Father's mysterious force that we now turn in order to more perfectly comprehend the manner in which the human spirit of Christ inter-penetrates our own human spirit in order to be present with us as we make our journey into the freedom Father intends. I recently received the following insightful email at the very time I was attempting to explain and set forth the concept of the *spirit of Christ:*

> *I have just read your May Lifechangers newsletter about the human Spirit of our Lord has been given to each of those born into His Kingdom. I am pondering that a bit and certainly believe there is truth in that since Paul's writings are full of references to all of who we are in Christ but also "Christ in you, the hope of glory." I am a retired Professor of Mechanical Engineering and have done considerable research in the area of stress analysis, fracture, etc. One of the areas I have worked in involves the use of holography. Your note reminded me of something I think would interest you.*
>
> *With a proper setup I can make a hologram of anything, pictures, words, etc. on a glass plate. This involves setting a specific angle of incidence of the laser ray onto the plate. To view the message, picture, etc. involves a particular setup where the exact same angle of the single*

wavelength ray is passed through the plate. The message becomes visible. If I change the incident angle slightly I can now store a second message, and a third and in fact entire books on the same plate of glass. The only thing lost is some intensity but in the spiritual application I am confident that the Lord has adequate intensity for the task. Each of these 'pages' can then be recalled by passing a ray back through the plate at the proper angle. I hope this is fairly clear. The bottom line is that on a single holographic plate we can store entire volumes of books.

*The next step relates to your note in the newsletter. If I take a small segment of that plate, just break it off. On that small segment **I have the entire amount of information still stored—all of it. I have removed nothing from the original plate.***

The point is, if the Lord can provide a way for us to do something such as that, we can see His intent.

God's intent has always been to inter-penetrate our human spirit with the human spirit of Christ so that we can make this journey to freedom!

Next, we will look at how Jesus' human spirit was prepared to be the Way to please the Father.

How Do We Learn to Please the Father?

> But if one loves God truly [with affectionate reverence, prompt obedience, and grateful recognition of His blessing], **he is known by God** [recognized as worthy of His intimacy and love, and he is owned by Him]. [Yes. We can know Him and He desires to know us] (1 Cor. 8:3).

> You have received a spirit of adoption as sons by which we cry out, "Abba! Father!" (Rom. 8:15).

I hope to communicate a unique and increasingly *relational* insight into the Person of Christ that has for several months been repeatedly illuminated to me. We all have needed to see Christ more as the Way to His Father than as an established goal to be attained. We are seeking to emphasize and not categorize so this in no way diminishes the function of the Holy Spirit.

The Apostle Paul says it quite clearly: If we love God…we are *known* by Him (see 1 Cor. 8:3). Knowing God has been a motivation for most of my life, and the idea of God as a Father getting to know me gives fresh emphasis. This illumination has rekindled my love for God and helped me understand that Jesus has been assigned to take me to the Father as stated clearly in John 14:6, "Jesus said to him, I am the way, and the truth, and the life; no one comes to the Father but through Me." Paul also says, "then I will *know* fully just as I also have been fully *known*" (1 Cor. 13:12). If God actually wants to know us and we surely want to know Him, what could possibly prevent that from happening? If we were clear and confident that it was Christ's job description to take us to the Father, we would better *cultivate* our relationship with Christ and release Him to prepare us more perfectly to understand the Father.

For years we've been working at understanding how the seven *communicable* DNA attributes of God[3] the Father have been designed to become ours. Now, we are asking the question: *How* does Jesus actually take us to the Father? He does it by mentoring and imparting to us His Own human spirit that has been matured and tested in the principles of the Kingdom that please the Father. The direct result of our following Christ is that by absorbing and embracing the spirit of Christ we are conformed to His image. He imparts to us His mind, His heart, and His motives so that we can

[3]The communicable attributes of God are compassion, gracious, slow to anger, mercy, truth, faithful, and forgiving. The noncommunicable attributes of God are Eternal, Spirit, Omniscient, Omnipresent, Omnipotent, and Immutable.

become a Father-pleaser in a similar manner as He was.

Listen as the writer to Hebrews explains Who this Jesus is and what He is concerned about:

> *⁶In burnt offerings and sin offerings You have taken no delight. ⁷Then I said, Behold, here I am, coming to do Your will, O God — [to fulfill] what is written of Me in the volume of the Book (Heb. 10:6-7).*

Father is expressing Himself to us in the Person of His Son saying that all of the accumulated religious activity is not what He desired. What He wants and what every Father desires is for His children to learn what *pleases* Him. It is not complicated, however, complications do arise in our human effort needed to make it happen. Paul made it clear in Philippians 2:13 that it is,

> *[Not in your own strength] for it is God Who is all the while effectually at work in you [energizing and creating in you the power and desire], both to will and to work for His good pleasure and satisfaction and delight.*

At the time the Lord was unfolding this to me, Judith and I traveled to Florida to spend a few days with my three sisters. My Mom and Dad divorced when I was 12 years old and life seemed to hand me the responsibility to be the surrogate father for my five sisters (two have since gone to be with the Lord). This has been an assignment of joy over the years and has served to help us all understand the Lord more perfectly. When we arrived, my older sister, Diane, now 86 years old, embraced us with such tenderness—as if to say, everything was going to be alright. We have been on a spiritual journey together for more than 70 years. She was, as many of you will remember, the person responsible for my originally coming to Christ at age 12 and again at age 24.

We had a wonderful visit at the kitchen table where I opened what I was seeing about the *spirit of Christ* (note the small s in spirit). To my amazement, I discovered that there are no fixed rules to determine whether the word spirit (*ruach* or *pneuma*) are to be capitalized except by the context. When I attempted to see how this was set forth in the Scripture, I was simply over-whelmed––I found more than 2400 references to spirit, some with capitals and many without! What we are discovering has been stated with impact by Albert Einstein when he said,

> *Every one who is seriously involved in the pursuit of science becomes convinced that a spirit is manifest in the laws of the Universe-a spirit vastly superior to that*

*of man, and one in the face of which we
with our modest powers must feel humble.*

Rather casually, I asked my three sisters if it was possible that on the Cross, at the moment of His death, *Jesus offered His Own human spirit to God the Father.* Of course, all that Christ experienced and everything that occurred was born and facilitated by the Person of the Holy Spirit in preparation for this Eternal Lamb to be made a sin-offering. What I wanted to distinguish had to do with giving up *His Own human spirit.* At the end of our family sharing time, none of us wanted to talk; we just sat there in the consciousness of God's Own Presence. *We were all aware, without discussion or addition, that Jesus had given Himself to each of us in more of a relational way than we had ever considered.*

I cannot deny others the *authentic* experience I had in spite of the risk of criticism that I could be distorting the Person of Christ or doing something that was not biblical. It takes a sincere effort to gain *experiential* understanding of Who He as a Man in order to follow Him and *know* the Father. I hold no strange or unorthodox Christology but all doctrinal definitions are pitifully inadequate. Listen to Matthew's doctrinal pre-supposition concerning this subject:

> *All things have been entrusted and delivered to Me by My Father; and **no one** fully knows and accurately understands*

*the Son except the Father, and **no one**
fully knows and accurately understands
the Father except the Son and anyone to
whom the Son deliberately wills to make
Him known (Matt 11:27).*

What God is saying is that there are *dimensions*
to the Person of Christ and insights into the nature
of the Father that He has chosen not to reveal at
this time. I can handle that. That certainly makes
me more comfortable and motivated than thinking
I know it all!

We have all been taught the basic assumption
that Jesus became the Lamb, gave His life on
the Cross, and went back to Heaven so that the
Holy Spirit could come to take His place. This
premise may be theoretically correct, however,
when we seek to make the relational application,
there might be more to this process than we have
understood. The realm of the Spirit/spirit may
not fit into neat categories. What we are seeking
to communicate may be more *soteriological* (how
salvation is accomplished) than *Christological*
(explanation of the nature of Christ). What I saw
was very *relational*—Christ *Himself* loves me and,
wonder of wonders, wants to be with me! This is
what John 17:24 says, "Father, I desire that those
whom You have given me, be with me where I am."
*Christ has not only demonstrated His love for us, He
has made intricate arrangements to participate with*

us, be present with us, and be our source of strength on our personal journey into God.

This seems extraordinarily important because what is at stake is a more relational and functional insight into how God designed the redemptive act to *bring us to Himself.* Somehow, we must find a way to get beyond our present application that Jesus' sacrifice was *limited* to my forgiveness. He gave *Himself* to us in every possible way—even in the complexities and crazies that life presents for the working out of our salvation. He gives Himself *for me* as the sacrificial Lamb of God, and He gives His human spirit *to me* in order to conform me into the image of Himself. Christ's human spirit already gained Father's pleasure (see Matt. 3:17, 17:5). Christ successfully pleased the Father so that success also belongs to us as His Bride because Jesus Christ and His Bride are one spirit.

Christ promised to be *with me*—never to leave me and never forsake me. His *personal presence* becomes an uninterrupted source of life. He is the major reason we even have the ability to *abide* and bring forth the fruit of the Spirit that Father is expecting (see John 15:8). All that comes under the heading of "maturity" must be understood as our being conformed to the image of Jesus Christ. *Everything* is, of course, born in and administered by the Holy Spirit Who *takes the things of Christ and reveals them to us.* Father asks that we see Christ as being present with us, caring and moving on our behalf to impart life, strength, and a heart of obedience so that we can please the Father as He did in His Own life and ministry! Christ speaks of our *inheriting* with Him and from Him all that Father has promised. Living in His presence is the normal Christian life! This pivotal point may be made more applicable if we reversed it: God was *personally present* in Christ as 2 Corinthians 5:19 states:

> *It was God [personally present] in Christ, reconciling and restoring the world to favor with Himself, not counting up and holding against [men] their trespasses [but cancelling them], and committing to us the message of reconciliation (of the restoration to favor).*

Christ is *personally present* in me and you. It is not only the Holy Spirit but Christ's human spirit that *dwells in our heart by faith*. Such clarity enables us to see and experience Christ *breathing* His very life into us as His personal gift. As a consequence, we begin to perceive, depend, and call upon Him as One Who is far more involved with us than we may have formerly understood. The spirit of Christ understood in this manner makes Him more intercessory, more caring, and more compassionate toward us in actually assisting us to make our journey. Hebrews 2:16 makes this clear,

For because He Himself [in His humanity] has suffered in being tempted (tested and tried), He is able [immediately] to run to the cry of (assist, relieve) those who are being tempted and tested and tried [and who therefore are being exposed to suffering].

The very idea seems to make us more Christ-centered! We are enabled to draw more effectively upon all that Jesus provided through His Own obedience to the Father.

The Breath of God

The breath of God is the solitary life source; in His very breath (*ruach/pneuma*) is the Spirit/spirit of Life that dwells in Christ Jesus. Christ imparts His spirit to us through His breath. When Christ breathed upon the disciples, that *breath* became the authority and life source by which they were able to forgive, heal, impart, and strengthen others. The Latin word *esse,* from which we gain the word *essence* or being, may help us understand this. Jesus' Own human spirit is the *essence* of His Person, the very Person whom He has prepared to give to us to be with us unto the end of the age! Like the Apostle Paul said, "I am with you in *spirit*" (small 's') (1 Cor. 5:4; Col. 2:5). It is the very breath of Jesus that is with us.

Life and death are in the breath of God. Paul says "the Lord Jesus will slay him with the breath of His mouth" (2 Thess. 2:8). He also gives *life* by the breath of His mouth: "For the law of the Spirit (spirit) of life [which is] in Christ Jesus [the law of our new being] has freed me from the law of sin and of death" (Rom. 8:2). The new creation and the One New man of Christ's creation were both created by Christ's *breathing* upon them. Mark 15:37, "And Jesus uttered a loud cry, and breathed out His life." John 20:22, "And having said this, He breathed on them and said to them, receive the Holy Spirit!"

It is Christ Who seeks to *conform me to His Own image* in order for me to become more *pleasing* to God as a Father. He has not simply turned me over to the Scripture (*logos*) and/or human will power. He has not left me in some intellectual/philosophical no-mans-land. He has come *Himself* to bring me to His Father. Acknowledging His immediate and existential involvement in my own person may serve as an added source of enablement, strengthening the Person of the Holy Spirit and giving added impartation to the one who seems to be most unsteady, questioning or even considering the unthinkable thought of *turning back, after having put our hand to the plow.*

Jesus Christ has given Himself to us continually and without interruption in order to breath His life into us. He has come to enable us to respond to every demand or expectation of the Father. His life becomes our life. His breath is our breath. His purpose is our purpose. He seeks to *impart* His very thinking process so that we actually have the mind of Christ (see 1 Cor. 2:16)!

It is the very presence of Jesus, Himself, that constitutes the journey into becoming one with the Father as stated in John 10:30, "I and the Father are one [heart and mind]." The application is not complicated: As I fully commit to follow Jesus, His human spirit is joined to my human spirit and I am moved toward alignment with the mind of Christ, which is needed for me to be one with the Father. Jesus has given His very person so that I can have my own *ABBA, Father* encounter with God.

The Self-Emptying Spirit of Christ

If Jesus is our Source, just how did He prepare Himself to make His Own human spirit, including His love of and absolute obedience to the Father, available to us?

The human spirit of Jesus was affected by the Holy Spirit at His conception and birth, He was *impacted* at His water baptism, born of the Spirit in a manner analogous to our own. The Holy Spirit, of course, is the energizer and guard. He is the guide, the One Who nourishes and the One Who takes the very Person of Jesus Christ to the hurting world. Jesus said, "the Son can do nothing of Himself, unless it is something He sees the Father doing; for whatever the Father does, these things the Son also does in like manner" (John 5:19). He has engaged and embraced what is identified as *kenotic love—Agape* that empties itself on behalf of others. It is that love that Christ wants to impart to every believer in order to bring them to maturity. He is the Way to that freedom, which no one else can offer. His job description is to take us to the Father!

At Christ's baptism, the Holy Spirit came upon *the spirit of Christ* for the purpose of taking the redemptive act out into the hurting world:

> *This is eternal life, that they may know You, the only true God, and Jesus Christ whom You have sent" (John 17:3).*

> *I in them and You in Me, that they may be perfected in unity, so that the world may know that You sent Me, and loved them, even as You have loved Me (John 17:23).*

The emphasis on eternal life is more than uninterrupted time spent in Heaven! Throughout Scripture Paul makes it clear that in the fullness of time all things in the heavens and on the earth were summed up in Christ (see Eph. 1:10). He refers to being full of the *spirit* of Christ in Acts 6:3, "Therefore, brethren, select from among you seven men of good reputation, full of the *spirit* and of wisdom, whom we may put in charge of this task." In Acts 6:8, He refers to the spirit of Stephen being "full of grace and power, was performing great wonders and signs among the people." Contrast this with Paul's references to the Holy Spirit in Acts 7:55, "But being full of the Holy Spirit, he gazed intently into heaven and saw the glory of God, and Jesus standing at the right hand of God." It is the presence of Christ that made Stephen willing to embrace martyrdom and do it with the same attitude and ambiance that did Jesus when it was His time to obey the Father. It is Jesus Who said:

> *I have made Your Name known to them and revealed Your character and Your very Self, and I will continue to make [You] known, that the love which You have bestowed upon Me may be in them [felt in their hearts] and that I [Myself] may be in them! (John 17:26).*

Then, when Jesus offered the Father His human spirit, He cried out with a loud voice and said, "'Father, into Your hands I commit My spirit.' Having said this, He breathed His last" (Luke 23:46; Psa. 31:6). It was Jesus' Own human spirit, one that with much suffering, conflict, and personal cost was brought to perfection and emerged as the perfectly mature human being known as the Son of Man. That human spirit is all that He is past, present, and future. Father transformed Christ's human spirit into the source of perfection as an example of all that is pleasing to Him as well as the source of future intercession and enablement in order to bring us all to Himself. 2 Corinthians 5:19 states that "it was God [personally present] in Christ, reconciling and restoring the world to favor with Himself, not counting up and holding against [men] their trespasses [but cancelling them], and committing to us the message of reconciliation (of the restoration to favor)." The intended purpose of the entire redemptive act was so that He could be personally present in His Own people for the purpose of bringing us to His Father (see John 17:26).

The following three verses have one theme: It is the *spirit of Jesus* that is the source of life and personal victory. Please read them carefully and allow to them to speak for themselves, not forcing a meaning that we have previously assumed or have already placed upon them:

> *That the God of our Lord Jesus Christ, the Father of glory, may give to you a **spirit** of wisdom and of revelation in the knowledge of Him (Eph. 1:17).*

> *For I know that this will turn out for my deliverance through your prayers and the provision of the S(s)spirit of Jesus Christ (Phil. 1:19).*

Seeking to know what person or time the Spirit/spirit of Christ within them was indicating as He predicted the sufferings of Christ and the glories to follow (1 Pet. 1:11).

Father received Christ's human *spirit* that constituted the eternal, uncreated, incorruptible Seed and inseminated that Seed into us in the New Birth. This means we now have in our own person the two natures (human/divine) intermingled but unmixed. It took the church fathers years of conflict and agony to work out Who Christ is and what He does in order to see the two natures unmixed. Now we can understand the creeds of Christendom: He originated fully divine as the Son of God and as a human took on the Seed of Abraham and became fully human.

Paul says that in the fullness of time, God took the spirit of His Son and gave it to us (see Gal. 4:6). I have never thought along those lines, but when I saw it, it felt like some type of transcendent sensation had taken place. Paul is *actually* saying that God the Father gave us the human spirit of Christ to bring us to Himself! That means it is not only a one-time experience but is progressive and incremental. Galatians 4:1-7 says the same:

[1] Think of it this way. If a father dies and leaves an inheritance for his young children, those children are not much

*better off than slaves until they grow up, even though they actually own everything their father had. ²They have to obey their guardians until they reach whatever age their father set. ³And that's the way it was with us before Christ came. We were like children; we were slaves to the basic spiritual principles of this world. ⁴But when the right time came, God sent his Son, born of a woman, subject to the law. ⁵God sent him to buy freedom for us who were slaves to the law, so that he could adopt us as his very own children. ⁶And because we are his children, **God has sent the Spirit/spirit of his Son into our hearts, prompting us to call out, "Abba, Father." ⁷**Now you are no longer a slave but God's own child. And since you are his child, God has made you his heir.*

Abba, Father

"Abba Father" is a statement that moves us toward personal freedom. George MacDonald, of whom C. S. Lewis said he didn't know anyone closer to Christ than MacDonald, wrote a book entitled *The Hope of the Gospel.*[4] In it he said that the word *adoption* has been totally distorted and

---

[4]MacDonald, George. *The Hope of the Gospel.* © 2007 BiblioBazaar, pg.104, 105. ISBN 978-1-4346-1422-3

does *not* signify the process of our being adopted at all:

> *Adoption is no translation of the word at all for which it stands. The Greek signifies the **Father's recognition**, when he comes of age, of the child's relation to Him, by giving him his fitting place of dignity in the house; I repeat, the word has nothing to do with the process of adoption, **it means the manifestation of the grown up sons.***

As the result of Father having sent the spirit of His Son into our hearts (see Gal. 4:6), we are free from being *preoccupied* with ourselves. This, as I understand it, is some kind of spiritual experience or encounter. The direct result is a jubilant heart-cry that sounds like: "ABBA," "Father" or "Father, My Father". It is a discovery, an illumination, an insight that no one can possibly take from you. My sense of this kind of a happening will become *increasingly* necessary because globally we are moving toward a climate of rejection of the message of Christ and His Love.

A helpful reference to "ABBA, Father" comes from *The Forgotten Father*,[5] the book I recommended earlier:

---

[5]Smail, Thomas. (1980, 1996). *The Forgotten Father*. Paternoster Press, p. 146. ISBN #0-340-25365-7.

The essence of sonship is trustful obedience— if one thing has emerged from our study, it is that Abba is a Gethsemane word spoken by the Son made man who trusts his Father to absolutely that he can obey him completely. His call to sonship of the Eternal Son consists of a divine obedience. **The sonship of the adopted human sons of a human obedience. Gospel obedience is a response to God's grace and not its condition.** *The way of Law says: "If you obey, God will receive you as his son." The way of the Gospel says: "God has received you as his sons, just as you are in all of your unworthiness. Your response to that is to obey. It is our obedience that keeps us close to him!"*

I have attempted to present Christ as having given His *human* spirit as the continual *source* of life and divine encounters in which Father chooses to reveal Himself to us in ways that are above our understanding. Hebrews 12:2 makes this very clear:

Looking away [from all that will distract] to Jesus, Who is the **Leader and the Source of our faith** *[giving the first incentive for our belief] and is also it's Finisher [bringing it to maturity and perfection]. He, for the joy [of obtaining*

the prize] that was set before Him,
endured the cross, despising and ignoring
the shame, and is now seated at the right
hand of the throne of God.

The phrase "bringing it to maturity and perfection" is the Greek word *telios,* which has been a personal comfort and strength to me for many years. It is a beautiful word used some 26 times in the New Testament. It states that Jesus is both the beginner or originator of our faith and He is also the One Who brings it to completion, maturity, or *telios*!

What It Means to Yield Our Human Spirit

Shall we not much more cheerfully submit
to the Father of spirits and so [truly] live?
(Heb. 12:9).

At the freeway entrance sat a small car with driver who was intimidated by the sheer speed and volume of the freeway traffic. Behind that car sat a boisterous and impatient driver who suddenly shouted out the window: "The sign says YIELD, not give up!"

It is much easier to give up than to yield. It has taken me a lifetime to even begin to learn that, and at 84 years old, I feel like I now need to cram for my finals! As I continue to understand how Christ's human spirit brings us to maturity so that we can know the Father, I am mindful that we must prepare ourselves for that specific moment when we breathe our last and pass into the very presence of our Lord. There are three significant and helpful passages of Scripture that provide insights on how to yield:

> *Into Your hands I commit my spirit; You have redeemed me, O Lord, the God of truth and faithfulness (Ps. 31:5).*

> [59]*And while they were stoning Stephen, he prayed, Lord Jesus,* **receive and accept and welcome my spirit!** [60]*And falling on his knees, he cried out loudly, Lord, fix not this sin upon them [lay it not to their charge]! And when he had said this, he fell asleep [in death]. This is Stephen's mature and most needed example. When understood and embraced, becomes preparatory (Acts 7:59-60).*

> *And Jesus, crying out with a loud voice, said, Father, into Your hands I commit My spirit! And with these words, He expired (Luke 23:49).*

It may be well worth the effort to practice yielding to the circumstances of life. Presently, I am doing what I am requesting of you—often repeating and practicing the response of Father, into your hands, I commit my human spirit! I am doing it verbally when possible and quietly when the circumstance require it. Such a verbal practice and intentional yielding of our human spirit results in personal discipline that moves us toward the Father and results in personal freedom.

LIFECHANGERS®

P.O. Box 3709 ❖ Cookeville, TN 38502
931.520.3730 ❖ lc@lifechangers.org

Other *Plumblines* by Bob Mumford
Available through Lifechangers, Amazon or Barnes & Noble

Acting Against Myself

Acting against myself (AAM is the proper way to live our Christian life. It has to do with distinguishing between light and dark, Agape and Eros, so that we can leave the old way of life and live differently. Agape is behavioral. It isn't legal or methodical; it needs to be brought out of the court room into the family room. An Agape reformation begins by learning to act against ourselves. Agape alone expects and requires us to mature to the point of being able to give ourselves away. In Matthew 16:24-25, Jesus states this as "forgetting himself and his own interests." Christ discipled the twelve, incrementally teaching them what it meant to act against themselves. He taught them and us both by example and by biblical precept. ISBN 1-884004-94-6

It Came to Pass

Change is inevitable. In this Plumbline, Bob explains how the whole world has been plunged into rapid and intense change since the 1960s. Making course corrections can be compared to sailing; we must "tack" into change little bits at a time, often seeming to be off course even though we are heading in the right direction. A look back at the Body of Christ and historical events over the last few decades will illustrate this "tacking" process more clearly. ISBN 1-884004-95-4

Journey to the Father on the Agape Road

This Plumbline is an agridged version of the book The Agape Road and contains the essential principles of the book. From deep and agonizing personal experience, Bob shares his victory of three life-crippling hindrances: anger, a critical mouth, and free-floating anxiety. The principles that worked for him will work for you, too—no matter what private issues you may be struggling with. After years of pastoring, preaching, counseling, and writing, Bob shares how you can fulfill your destiny by escaping the seven giants of failure, learning how to rest on the Agape Road, experiencing the healing power of Agape, and discovering the joy of being a Father-pleaser. Reading Journey to the Father is like sitting at the feet of the Master, feeling His words deep in your heart, and sensing His healing power in the broken places of your life. ISBN 1-884004-98-9.

The Trap, Exit and Reward

Using two stories about the trap, Bob identifies what keeps us trapped and how to get out. While we are in the trap we continually surrender our freedom for our feelings. The entire creation waits to be set free from its slavery to corruption into freedom (see Rom. 8:19-21). From 2 Peter 1, Bob shows us six steps to finding the exit and the reward: a rich and abundant welcome into the eternal kingdom of our Lord (2 Pet. 1:11) so that we can participate in setting creation free. ISBN 978-1-940054-01-8

Feed My Sheep: 60 Years in Ministry

1954 to 2014 marks 60 years in active ministry for Bob Mumford. His story began in the Navy in a little four-bed sick bay on the USS Aludra when he began to embrace the call to teach. Feeding God's people in every nation has been his life-long commission. This story chronicles Bob's journey from meeting Christ through his Navy experience, Bible College, Charismatic Renewal, and the Covenant Movement. He shares what he has learned in following Jesus all these years. ISBN 978-1-940054-05-6

Circle of Friendship

Within the Trinity of the Father, Son, and Holy Spirit there is a circle of friendship, and we are being invited into it. When Jesus started His journey with the disciples, one of His goals was friendship—He wanted to reveal Father's secrets to them. Real friendship involves trust and intimacy, not over-familiarity. In this Plumbline, Bob gives us four ingredients common to friendship and shows us the importance of relationships being reciprocal. God is calling us into a true friendship with Himself and with others. We must accept each other just like we are and choose to surrender self-protection and control. When we center our whole being on pleasing the Father, it radically affects our ethical and moral behavior. A vital aspect of our circle of friendship with God is waiting on Him; by it we exchange our weakness for His strength. After a while, we come to a place where the poise of our soul is toward the Lord, and we can enjoy Father's presence. ISBN 978-1-940054-06-3

LIFECHANGERS®

P.O. Box 3709 ❖ Cookeville, TN 38502
931.520.3730 ❖ lc@lifechangers.org

www.ingramcontent.com/pod-product-compliance
Lightning Source LLC
Chambersburg PA
CBHW071748020426
42331CB00008B/2230